Saturdays with Pop

Jane Langford
Illustrated by Ron Mahoney

Rigby

A Harcourt Achieve Imprint

www.Rigby.com
1-800-531-5015

Literacy by Design Leveled Readers: *Saturdays with Pop*

ISBN-13: 978-1-4189-3789-8
ISBN-10:   1-4189-3789-4

Printed in China
1A 2 3 4 5 6 7 8 985 13 12 11 10 09 08 07

Contents

CHAPTER 1
Pop's Study

Saturdays were special. On Saturdays Seb visited Granddad and Pop. Pop was Granddad's father and was a very old man. They lived together in a big house that was even older than Pop.

Seb's favorite place in the big old house was Pop's study. The study was not empty and did not echo like the rest of the house. It was dark and warm and snug. The shelves that lined the room were filled with models that Pop had made when he was a young man. Seb loved to look at the models and talk about them with Pop.

But one Saturday when Seb arrived at the house, Pop was not there to greet him.

"He went to bed," said Granddad. "He's not feeling well."

Seb was disappointed. He had looked forward to spending time with Pop. Now what would he do?

"Don't worry," said Granddad. "Pop will be all right. Go into the study on your own. Just be careful not to break anything!"

Seb had never been in the study on his own before. He peeked around the door, then quietly tiptoed inside. The room was pin-drop silent. Seb sat in Pop's huge green armchair. The chair almost swallowed him up in leathery softness. He sat in the center of the chair's big green mouth, hugging his knees to his chest.

Seb's eyes scanned the shelves. He knew the detail of every model, and if he shut his eyes, he could see them as clearly as if he were looking at a photograph.

As always, Seb's eyes were drawn to his favorite model. It was a ship. But this wasn't just any ship–this ship was very special. It was a magnificent ship in a bottle.

The ship stood in the center of Pop's old oak desk. Seb never got tired of looking at it. He never understood how Pop had managed to fit such a big ship into such a little bottle. The sails were so tall that they touched the top of the bottle, but the mouth of the bottle was tiny. It was hardly big enough to put your little finger in. Not that Seb had ever tried, of course.

Seb wasn't usually allowed to touch the models, but today was different. He was all alone. No one would know if he picked the bottle up–just for a quick look.

Seb lifted the bottle carefully in his hands and held it to his eye, measuring the size of the sails against the size of the bottle's mouth. Seb felt the cool, smooth glass of the bottle in his fingertips.

"How on earth did Pop ever get the ship in there?" he wondered.

Suddenly the bottle slipped. It didn't fall, but the ship inside the bottle was jolted. The magnificent tall sails unexpectedly fell over. Instead of standing tall and proud, the loose yellow canvas flopped untidily over the hull of the ship.

Seb couldn't believe his eyes. He quickly tipped the bottle upside down, hoping that the sails would fall back into the correct position, but of course they didn't. The topsy-turvy contents of the bottle simply became more jumbled than ever.

CHAPTER 2
What a Disaster!

Seb was terrified. He put the bottle down, then immediately picked it up again. What should he do? He took a deep breath to steady himself. He had to fix this mess and quickly! Somehow he had to reach the sails to mend them.

"I'll get the cork out of the neck of the bottle first," he thought. "Then I'll be able to reach the sails."

The cork came out of the bottle easily, but the neck of the bottle was narrow and long. Seb explored it carefully with his little finger, but he couldn't reach the tangled remains of the sails. Seb started to panic.

"Stay calm," he told himself. "Stay calm!"

Seb's eyes swept the room as he searched for a tool to reach into the mouth of the bottle. He saw a pen on the desk and picked it up.

Very carefully, Seb pushed the pen into the bottle. Great! It went in, no trouble! He pushed it a little further, and it reached the sails!

Seb pushed the pen against the sails trying to lift them upward. He tried again and again, but it was no use. The pen just poked uselessly at the heap of material. He couldn't lift the sails back up.

Seb sighed and withdrew the pen from the neck of the bottle. But, as he did so, he saw that the yellowed sails were now covered with dots of blue ink. What a disaster!

"They're ruined!" wailed Seb.

From the kitchen, Granddad called to Seb.

Seb froze. What should he do? He quickly thrust the bottle into the bottom drawer of the oak desk.

Granddad called again, so Seb ran to the kitchen. His cheeks were flushed and he fought back tears.

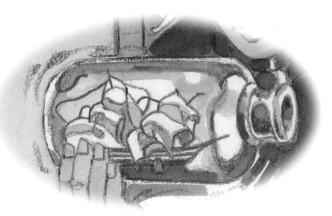

Granddad handed him a tray. "Take
Pop his lunch, will you please, Seb?"

Seb nodded silently and hastily backed
out of the door. The thick, buttery smell
of the soup made his stomach turn.

Pop was dozing, so Seb gently laid
the tray on his bedside table.

"Pop," he whispered, "your lunch is ready."

Pop opened one eye and mumbled his thanks.

Seb stepped out of the room and fled back down the hall to the study.

Granddad stopped him. "Seb," he said, "what's wrong?"

"Nothing!" said Seb quickly.

Granddad lifted Seb's chin, and looked straight into his tear-filled eyes. "Seb," he repeated, "what's wrong?"

Teardrops fell down Seb's cheeks.

Seb took Granddad's hand. He led him into the study and opened the desk drawer.

"Oh, Seb!" exclaimed Granddad.

"I didn't mean to!" said Seb. "It slipped in my hands and the whole thing caved in."

Granddad picked up the bottle. He took a long look inside. "It's very old," he said, "and it's a bit fragile, like Pop and me."

Seb smiled weakly. "You're not fragile!" he said.

Granddad smiled back. "No, maybe not, but Pop isn't strong. He will be upset about this."

Seb rubbed the sleeve of his sweater over his tear-smudged face. "Can we fix it?" he asked.

Granddad shook his head. "Well, Seb, I don't know. I never had the patience for fiddling around with these models." He paused briefly. "But I guess I did watch Pop make an awful lot of these. I suppose we could give it a try."

CHAPTER 3
Tweezers, Vinegar, and Thread

Granddad went to the garage to get a few things. He came back to the study with a pair of tweezers, a bottle of vinegar, some black cotton thread, and a spool of nylon thread.

"What are we going to do with those?" asked Seb.

Granddad peered at Seb over the rim of his glasses. "You'll find out!" he said.

Seb perched on the edge of his stool and watched Granddad as he worked with the silence and skill of a doctor.

Granddad gently pulled the cork out of the bottle and laid it on the desk next to the tweezers. His thick, stubby fingers reached out for the tweezers, but missed and knocked them onto the floor.

"Doctors don't do that," thought Seb. He leapt from his stool and rescued the tweezers for Granddad.

Granddad tried again, reaching into the bottle with the tweezers. He grasped the hull of the boat and pulled.

Seb gasped. The hull slipped easily out of the neck of the bottle. Hooray! But it dragged behind a terrible tangle of sails and rigging. Oh, no!

Granddad laid the wreckage on the desk. The once-white sails were yellowed with age. Long pieces of black thread lay tangled among them.

"What are those black pieces of thread?" asked Seb.

Granddad sighed, "It used to be the rigging."

"It's like a spider's web," said Seb.

Granddad swept his hand across the desk, scooped up the mess of sails and rigging, and dumped it into the trashcan.

"No!" cried Seb. "You can't do that!"

Granddad said, "We can't mend that tangled wreck."

"Then what are we going to do?" asked Seb hopelessly.

"We're going to make some new sails," said Granddad firmly. "Can you sew?"

Seb nodded.

"Good," said Granddad, "because I don't think my fingers are steady enough for the job."

Granddad pulled a clean white handkerchief out of his pocket and laid it on the desk. "This will do," he said. Then he rescued the old sails from the trash can and used them as a pattern to draw around.

Seb found a pair of scissors. He carefully cut around the lines that Granddad had drawn on the handkerchief. Granddad showed Seb how to roll the edge of the material between his thumb and forefinger to make a little hem.

"Now, sew that," he told Seb, "and keep those stitches tiny."

Seb did as he was told—his stitches looked like little dashes.

While Seb was busy sewing, Granddad cut several lengths of black thread. "This will be the new rigging!" he said.

21

CHAPTER 4
Side by Side

Seb and Granddad worked side by side for the rest of the afternoon. As soon as Seb finished sewing a sail, Granddad attached the rigging. There were several sails to be fixed. At last they were all done.

"Now we must attach the sails to the mast," said Granddad. He used the black threads to join the new white sails to the tall, proud mast.

"I think that's it!" said Granddad at last. "Except for the tricky part, of course."

Seb shuddered. "You mean putting the ship back in the bottle?"

Granddad nodded.

"Are we going to do that now?" Seb asked.

Granddad shook his head. "No," he replied. "There is something else I think we ought to do first."

Seb watched Granddad take the ship's bottle and carefully fill it with vinegar.

"What are you doing that for?" asked Seb in astonishment.

"To clean the glass!" replied Granddad. "It's as green as Pop's armchair! Age and dampness have caused that. You watch! This vinegar will soon clean it up."

Granddad was right. As he swirled the vinegar out of the bottle, the glass began to shine clean and bright.

"Now we'll let it dry," said Granddad. "It won't take long."

Granddad went to the kitchen to prepare dinner. Seb waited nervously in the study. He did not take his eyes off the ship because he was afraid it would collapse again.

When Granddad finally came back, they looked at the ship together. Then they looked at the bottle.

"It will never fit," whispered Seb.

"Yes it will," said Granddad. "Think positively!"

Granddad asked Seb to cut three pieces of nylon thread. The thread was so fine it was almost invisible.

Granddad tied one piece of thread to the top of the mast and attached the other two pieces to the corners of the two biggest sails.

"Those are the guide ropes," said Granddad.

"What are they for?" asked Seb.

"You'll see," said Granddad.

Granddad took hold of the sturdy little ship. His fingers went straight to a hinge at the bottom of the mast.

"I never knew there was a hinge there!" said Seb.

Granddad laughed. "That's the whole trick!" he said. "Watch!"

Granddad oiled the hinge, then folded the mast flat against the hull of the ship.

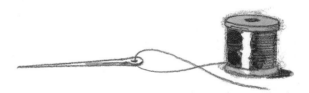

"Wow!" Seb was amazed. "So that's the secret! Now it can go in the bottle!"

"Not quite," said Granddad. "We have to fold up the sails first."

Granddad showed Seb how to fold the sails around the mast, making it as small and neat as possible.

28

"Now," said Granddad, "make sure that you keep hold of those guide ropes. We're lost without them!"

Seb still did not know what they were for, but he held them as if his life depended on it.

CHAPTER 5
The Tricky Part!

There was dead silence in the study. Granddad grabbed the stern of the ship between his finger and thumb. He used his little finger to keep the mast and the sails pressed firmly down. Then he slowly slid the ship into the mouth of the bottle.

Seb held his breath. *Please let it go in! Please let it go in!*

Granddad pushed the ship as far as it would go, but it wasn't far enough. The ship got trapped in the long, narrow neck of the bottle.

"Oh, no! It's stuck!" hissed Seb.

"No, it's not stuck," said Granddad. "My fingers are just too big. You try!"

Seb shook his head—he was scared.

"Go on! you can do it!"

Seb passed the guide ropes to Granddad. Then he gently took the ship and very carefully pushed it a little further into the bottle. He bit his lip and trembled.

"Don't be scared," said Granddad.

Seb tried again and pushed the ship all the way into the bottle. "Hooray!" he shouted.

The little ship sank calmly to the bottom of the bottle.

"Now," said Granddad, "let's see if we can raise the mast."

"Oh, I see! That's what the guide ropes are for!" whispered Seb.

Granddad did not say a word. He just began to pull the guide ropes.

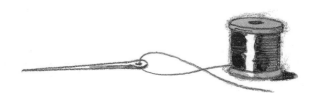

Gracefully, the mast slowly rose from the deck of the ship. Higher and higher it went until it touched the top of the bottle.

"Nearly there!" said Granddad.

He quickly put a rubber band around the neck of the bottle. It captured the guide ropes and the mast was held in place!

Seb shook with excitement. "That's it!" he squeaked. "That's it. You've done it!"

Granddad pushed the cork into the mouth of the bottle.

"No, *we've* done it!" he said victoriously.

CHAPTER 6
Not Such a Bad Day!

A voice called impatiently from Pop's room. "Hello. Is anybody there?"

Seb ran to Pop's room. "Sorry," he said, "we were just a little busy."

"Busy!" croaked Pop. "Well, I've been busy, too–busy sleeping! I feel much better now, and I'd like to get up."

Granddad helped Pop get dressed while Seb lingered in the doorway.

Pop looked at him suspiciously. "What have you been up to?" he asked.

Seb said nothing. He helped Pop get comfortable in his chair and wheeled him into the study.

Pop looked around and knew something was wrong. "What have you done?" he asked.

Granddad and Seb pointed at the ship. Pop stared for a moment, then coughed and spluttered as if he was going to choke. His face darkened, and Seb was frightened. Pop looked really upset.

But Granddad stood by his side. He nodded at the ship. "Looks like it did when I was a boy," Granddad said. "The sails are white and the glass is gleaming!"

Pop wheeled himself closer to the desk to study the ship. "This was my pride and joy," he said. "This was the first ship in a bottle that I ever made." He looked at Seb. "What happened?"

Seb looked into his great-granddad's eyes. His voice trembled as he spoke. "I'm sorry," he said. "I was looking at it, and I know I shouldn't have touched it, but I did. The bottle slipped in my hands and the rigging collapsed. Granddad helped me fix it."

"Did he now," said Pop, a smile just playing on his lips. "I could never get him interested in modelmaking when he was a boy."

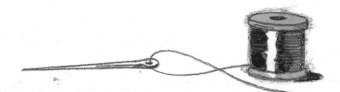

It was Granddad's turn to feel uneasy. "I was always interested," he said. "I was just more interested in watching than doing."

Pop turned to Seb. "And what about you, young man? Are you more interested in watching or doing?"

"Doing!" said Seb.

"Good!" said Pop. "You did a fine job on that ship."

Pop wheeled his chair around the desk. He nodded toward the shelves lined with aging models. "There are lots more over there that need mending."

Granddad laughed. "It looks as if your Saturdays are going to be very busy from now on, Seb!"

Seb smiled happily. Today hadn't turned out to be such a bad day after all. And from now on, he knew Saturdays were going to be fantastic!

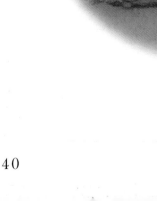